P9-DFR-650

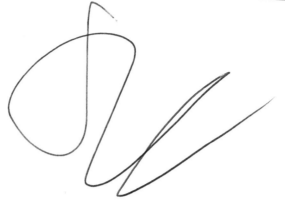

HERBIVORES

BY
S.L. HAMILTON

A&D Xtreme
An imprint of Abdo Publishing | abdopublishing.com

abdopublishing.com

Published by Abdo Publishing, a division of ABDO, PO Box 398166, Minneapolis, Minnesota 55439. Copyright ©2018 by Abdo Consulting Group, Inc. International copyrights reserved in all countries. No part of this book may be reproduced in any form without written permission from the publisher. A&D Xtreme™ is a trademark and logo of Abdo Publishing.

Printed in the United States of America, North Mankato, MN.
092017
012018

Editor: John Hamilton
Graphic Design: Sue Hamilton
Cover Design: Candice Keimig and Pakou Vang
Cover Photo: iStock
Interior Photos & Illustrations: Alamy-pgs 8-9, 12-13, 14-15, 18-19, 23 & 24-25; Deposit Photos-pgs 2-3, 4-5 & 11; Getty Images-pgs 10 & 20-21; iStock-pgs 1, 28-29, 30-31 & 32; Joschua Knüppe-pg 22; Science Source-pgs 6-7 & 26-27; Shutterstock-pgs 16-17.

Publisher's Cataloging-in-Publication Data

Names: Hamilton, S.L., author.
Title: Herbivores / by S.L. Hamilton.
Description: Minneapolis, Minnesota : Abdo Publishing, 2018. |
Series: Xtreme Dinosaurs |
    Includes online resources and index.
Identifiers: LCCN 2017946709 |
    ISBN 9781532112966 (lib.bdg.) |
    ISBN 9781532150821 (ebook)
Subjects: LCSH: Herbivores,
    Fossil--Juvenile literature. |
    Prehistoric animals--Juvenile
    literature. | Dinosaurs--
    Juvenile literature. |
    Paleontology--Juvenile
    literature.
Classification: DDC 567.9--dc23
LC record available at https://lccn.loc.gov/2017946709

Contents

HERBIVORES

Herbivores, or plant-eating dinosaurs, lived during the Mesozoic era. Most dinosaurs were plant eaters, but the largest are called sauropods. They died out 65 million years ago, but their fossils tell us these huge creatures were the biggest land animals to ever live. They weighed as much as 100 tons (91 metric tons). They stood more than 40 feet (12 m) tall, twice as tall as a giraffe. At 130 feet (40 m) in length, they were as long as two bowling alley lanes. Their massive size and strong muscles allowed them to live on Earth for 150 million years.

XTREME FACT – Sauropods were one of the most successful species to live on Earth. Their fossil remains have been found on every continent on the planet, including Antarctica.

TEETH

Sauropods had teeth made for eating plants. Some herbivores had spatula-shaped teeth that allowed them to eat tough vegetation. Others had peg-like teeth that they used to rake the leaves off trees.

Seismosaurus (Earthquake Lizard) with peg-like teeth.

Herbivores may not have chewed their food. They likely swallowed plants whole and allowed their massive stomachs to digest their meals over many days.

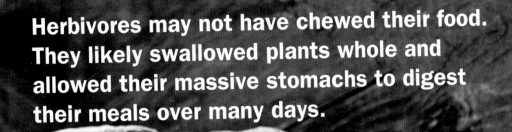

XTREME FACT – Sauropods had an unlimited supply of replacement teeth. Some species grew a new tooth every two weeks, while others replaced each tooth every two months.

NECKS

Sauropods had extremely long necks. The necks may have been used to reach the vegetation found at the tops of trees. Or the necks may have allowed sauropods to swing their heads from side-to-side, sucking up plants as they walked.

XTREME FACT – Scientists question whether sauropods held their heads up high (vertically). A sauropod would need a heart 15 times bigger than a whale's to pump blood up to their heads in that position. Many scientists believe they kept their heads at shoulder height, a horizontal position, and waved them back and forth to eat.

Giraffatitan brancai
(Giant Giraffe)

Legs and Feet

Sauropods had muscular legs. Most species had hind feet equipped with three claws. Scientists used to think the claws kept the huge dinosaurs from slipping on slick ground. However, claw marks do not show up in sauropod tracks. Paleontologists now believe that sauropods used their clawed back feet to scrape out nests on the ground.

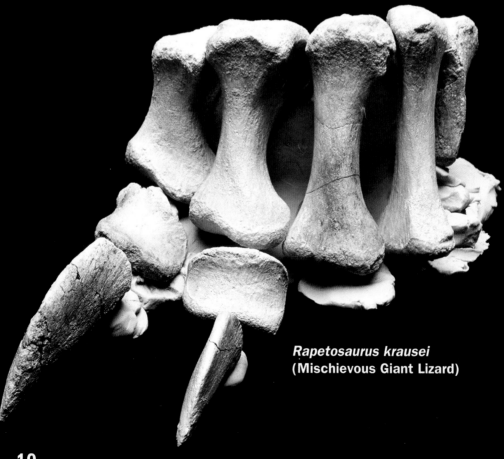

Rapetosaurus krausei
(Mischievous Giant Lizard)

Sauropods' front feet are called "hands." Early sauropods had one thumb claw on each hand. They may have used them to grip tree trunks as they reared up, or for ripping off leaves or branches. They may have been used for fighting or digging. However, as generations of sauropods lived and died, thumb claws grew smaller. Later sauropods did not have them at all.

TAILS

The long tails on sauropods were used to balance out their very long necks. The tail acted as an extra leg.

XTREME FACT – It was once thought that sauropods had a "butt brain." Fossil skeletons show an empty space near the hips. This led to the idea that the dinosaurs had a second brain in the rear that sped up messages from the main brain and helped them move their back legs and tail. However, this theory has been rejected. It's still unknown what filled that empty space.

The strong tails were likely used for defense. Sauropods could whip their tails back and forth with great power. Scientists believe that the tails could create a sound like the snap of a bullwhip. The noise may have been loud enough to break the sound barrier. The tail and its sounds would have frightened predators. It may also have been used to attract mates.

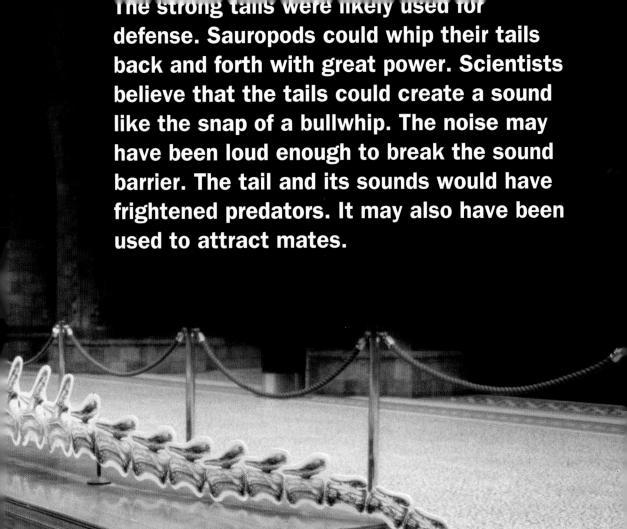

Argentinosaurus
(Argentine Lizard)

LARGEST SAUROPODS

Argentinosaurus lived 97 to 93.5 million years ago in today's South America. The massive beast grew up to 130 feet (40 m) in length and 65 feet (20 m) tall. It weighed up to 85 tons (77 metric tons). The first fossil remains were found in Argentina in 1987.

XTREME FACT – In 2014, one of the biggest sauropod fossils ever found was discovered by a farmer in the Patagonia region of Argentina, South America. It has not yet been named, but is part of a group of sauropods called titanosaurs. These massive beasts were the largest dinosaurs to walk the Earth. They outlived many of the other sauropods.

Alamosaurus is the largest sauropod found in North America. It lived about 69 million years ago. A few bones found in New Mexico suggest that the herbivore grew to a length of 131 feet (40 m) and weighed about 70 tons (63.5 metric tons). Scientists estimate its size based on these bones, but no one knows if the sauropod was full grown or still growing.

XTREME FACT – When a massive dinosaur died, it took a long time to be buried under dirt and vegetation. It was usually torn apart as a meal for predators. That is why a complete skeleton is seldom found.

Alamosaurus
(Ojo Alamo Formation Lizard)

LONGEST SAUROPODS

Diplodocus is one of the longest herbivore dinosaurs. Although not the heaviest sauropod, its very long neck and very long tail gave it an overall length of up to 150 feet (46 m). This is about the length of three semi-trailer trucks.

Diplodocus
(Double Beam)

Diplodocus, which means "double beam," is named for the extra bones on the underside of its tail. It lived in North America 154 to 152 million years ago.

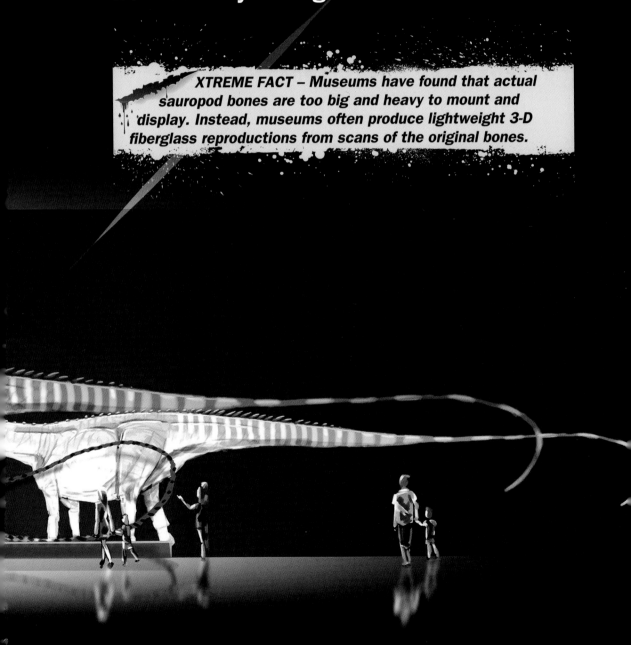

XTREME FACT – Museums have found that actual sauropod bones are too big and heavy to mount and display. Instead, museums often produce lightweight 3-D fiberglass reproductions from scans of the original bones.

LONGEST NECK

Mamenchisaurus lived in China 160 to 145 million years ago. This sauropod had the longest neck compared to its overall body size. Scientists estimate its neck length to be 30 feet (9 m). That is half of its body length of 60 feet (18 m).

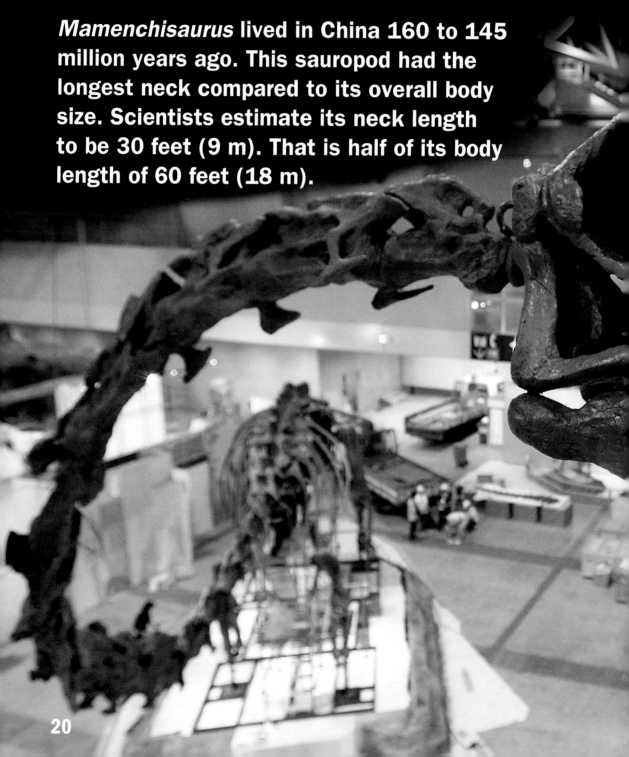

Mamenchisaurus
(Mamenchi Lizard)

SMALLEST SAUROPODS

The smallest adult sauropods are known as "dwarfs." *Ohmdenosaurus* lived in Germany about 183 to 174 million years ago. It reached a length of 13 feet (4 m). The dwarf sauropod weighed about 500 pounds (227 kg).

Ohmdenosaurus
(Ohmden Lizard)

Saltasaurus had the shortest neck and stubbiest legs of the known sauropods. It lived in South America about 70 million years ago. It was 42 feet (13 m) in length and weighed up to 7.6 tons (6.9 metric tons). Since it was not as big as most sauropods, it had small armored plates covering its back for protection.

Saltasaurus
(Lizard From Salta)

FAMOUS SAUROPODS

Brachiosaurus is one of the most famous of sauropods. It lived in North America about 156 to 151 million years ago. It weighed up to 62 tons (56 metric tons) and grew to a length of 82 feet (25 m). Unlike other sauropods, it had longer front legs than back legs. Scientists wonder if it could rear up on its hind legs to eat. At a height of up to 50 feet (15 m), it probably didn't need to.

**Brachiosaurus
(Arm Lizard)**

XTREME FACT – One of the most famous dinosaurs found by early fossil hunters was Brontosaurus (Thunder Lizard). As studies continued, it looked like it was really a type of Apatosaurus. In 2015, however, scientists again believe the famous dinosaur found in books, cartoons, and movies, may indeed have been its own species.

NESTING

Sauropods probably created above-ground nests in areas where Earth's heat would provide a very warm environment. They likely placed their nests near geysers or heat vents, or buried their eggs along with decaying vegetation that created warmth.

XTREME FACT – Female sauropods laid many small eggs. An egg was no bigger than a soccer ball.

Since sauropods' best form of protection was their immense size, the babies grew at an amazing rate of speed. Their birth weight was about the same as a human baby: 5.5 to 9.5 pounds (2.5 to 4.3 kilograms). Scientists guess that the babies doubled their weight in a week. As teenagers, they gained 4,409 pounds (2 metric tons) a year.

EXTINCTION

About 66 million years ago, a world-changing event occurred. It may have been an asteroid striking the Earth. Perhaps volcanoes began erupting. Climate may have changed. Diseases may have struck. Perhaps it was a number of things that caused the dinosaurs, including all the great sauropods, to die out. Fossil hunters continue to look for clues to explain what caused the extinction of these massive creatures whose

~~~~ the Earth.

GLOSSARY

BULLWHIP
A whip with a very long lash. Some sauropods' tails flicked like a bullwhip.

FOSSILS
The preserved remains or imprints of prehistoric animals or plants in stone.

GEYSER
A spring that shoots up hot water with explosive force from time to time.

HEAT VENT
An opening in the Earth's crust that allows the escape of heated gases, water, or air.

MESOZOIC ERA
A time in Earth's history from about 245 million to 65 million years ago. Dinosaurs roamed the Earth at this time. This overall era includes the Triassic, Jurassic, and Cretaceous periods.

PALEONTOLOGIST
A person who studies prehistoric fossil plants and animals.

PREDATOR
An animal that hunts, kills, and eats other animals.

Species

A group of living things that have similar looks and behaviors, but are not identical. They are often called by a similar name. For example, there are many species of sauropods.

Sound Barrier

When an object, such as an airplane, travels faster than the speed of sound, or about 768 miles per hour (343 meters per second) in dry air, it reaches the sound barrier. When this happens, an incredibly loud noise is created known as a sonic boom. It is believed that sauropod tails could whip fast enough to break the sound barrier and emit an explosive sonic boom.

Titanosaur

The largest of the sauropod dinosaurs, which included *Argentinosaurus*. These huge herbivores were the last sauropods to evolve and the last to die.

Online Resources

Booklinks
NONFICTION NETWORK
FREE! ONLINE NONFICTION RESOURCES

To learn more about Xtreme Dinosaurs, visit abdobooklinks.com. These links are routinely monitored and updated to provide the most current information available.

INDEX